★ ★

MONTANA

by Jonatha A. Brown

GARETH**STEVENS**
GS
P U B L I S H I N G
A Member of the WRC Media Family of Companies

Please visit our web site at: **www.garethstevens.com**
For a free color catalog describing Gareth Stevens Publishing's
list of high-quality books and multimedia programs, call
1-800-542-2595 (USA) or 1-800-387-3178 (Canada).
Gareth Stevens Publishing's fax: (414) 332-3567.

Library of Congress Cataloging-in-Publication Data

Brown, Jonatha A.
    Montana / Jonatha A. Brown.
      p. cm. — (Portraits of the states)
    Includes bibliographical references and index.
    ISBN-10: 0-8368-4702-4 — ISBN-13: 978-0-8368-4702-4 (lib. bdg.)
    ISBN-10: 0-8368-4719-9 — ISBN-13: 978-0-8368-4719-2 (softcover)
    1. Montana—Juvenile literature. I. Title. II. Series.
  F731.3.B75   2007
  978.6—dc22   2005036637

This edition first published in 2007 by
Gareth Stevens Publishing
A Member of the WRC Media Family of Companies
330 West Olive Street, Suite 100
Milwaukee, WI 53212 USA

This edition copyright © 2007 by Gareth Stevens, Inc.

Editorial direction: Mark J. Sachner
Project manager: Jonatha A. Brown
Editor: Catherine Gardner
Art direction and design: Tammy West
Picture research: Diane Laska-Swanke
Indexer: Walter Kronenberg
Production: Jessica Morris and Robert Kraus

Picture credits: Cover, © James P. Rowan; p. 4 © Nancy Carter/North
Wind Picture Archives; p. 5 © Corel; p. 6 © Kevin R. Morris/CORBIS;
p. 7 © Bettmann/CORBIS; p. 10 © North Wind Picture Archives; p. 11
© Gibson Stock Photography; pp. 12, 22 © Buddy Mays/CORBIS; pp. 15, 18,
21, 24 © John Elk III; pp. 16, 27 © Tom Bean; pp. 25, 29 © AP Images; p. 26
© Todd Kaplan/Idaho Stock Images; p. 28 © Mary Steinbacher/PhotoEdit

Printed in the United States of America

1 2 3 4 5 6 7 8 9 10 09 08 07 06

CONTENTS

Words that are defined in the Glossary appear
in **bold** the first time they are used in the text.

On the Cover: Glacier National Park is well known for its beauty. Here
you will find craggy peaks, green valleys, calm lakes, and lots of wildlife.

Introduction

Would you like to watch cowboys ride bucking broncos at a rodeo? Look at cave paintings that are thousands of years old? Hike along a mountain stream or ski down a powdery slope? You can do all of these things and more in Montana. This big state has something for almost everyone to enjoy.

Montana is in the northwestern United States. It lies just south of the Canadian border. The state is home to high craggy mountains and wide plains. At one time, Native Americans hunted buffalo and elk here. Later, miners, ranchers, and farmers took over the land. Today, Montana has plenty of room for all. It is a great place to live or visit.

Welcome to Montana!

Beautiful Bozeman Pass cuts through the Bridger Mountains in southern Montana.

The state flag of Montana.

MONTANA FACTS

- Became the 41st U.S. State: November 8, 1889
- Population (2004): 926,865
- Capital: Helena
- Biggest Cities: Billings, Missoula, Great Falls, Butte and nearby towns
- Size: 145,552 square miles (376,980 square kilometers)
- Nickname: The Treasure State
- State Tree: Ponderosa pine
- State Flower: Bitterroot
- State Animal: Grizzly bear
- State Bird: Western meadowlark

History

Native Americans have lived in Montana for a long time. They first came to the region thousands of years ago. These Native people hunted buffalo and other big animals. They lived in teepees and caves.

The First White Men

In 1682, the French claimed most of the land in this area. They began to explore it in 1743. That year, François and Louis Joseph de La Vérendrye became the first white men to reach Montana. They saw beaver and other animals. Later, they told other people about this land and the animals they saw there. Their stories drew more trappers and fur traders to Montana.

In 1803, France sold a huge amount of land to the United States. This land included the eastern part of Montana. The land sale was called the Louisiana Purchase.

Thousands of years ago, people painted pictures on the walls of caves. Today, you can see some of these pictures at Pictograph Caves State Park near Billings.

The U.S. government sent a group of men to explore its new land. The leaders of this group were Meriwether Lewis and William Clark. They headed west along the Missouri River. In 1805, the explorers found the source of the river in Montana. They kept going west to the Pacific Ocean. Then, they returned home by way of Montana. Along the way, Lewis and Clark saw many beavers and otters.

FUN FACTS

Giants of the Earth

Millions of years ago, dinosaurs lived in what is now Montana. Some of the huge creatures made nests and laid eggs in them. These dinosaurs may have been killed when a volcano erupted long ago. Today, **fossils** of dinosaurs and their eggs can be found near Choteau.

Lewis and Clark explored parts of Montana in 1805 and 1806. A Native woman named Sacagawea helped them. She acted as a guide and helped them talk with Natives they met along the way.

IN MONTANA'S HISTORY

Early Trading Posts

In 1807, Manuel Lisa built a trading post near the Bighorn River. He named it Fort Manuel Lisa. It was the first trading post in what is now Montana. Before long, many trading posts were built. Trappers brought animal **pelts** to the trading posts. There, they traded their pelts for tools, supplies, and other goods that they needed.

Killing Innocent People

In 1869, a small band of Natives stole a few horses and killed a white man near Fort Benton. This upset many white settlers. They went to the fort and asked the Army to take action. The leaders at Fort Benton blamed the Blackfoot tribe, so they sent soldiers to attack a Blackfoot village. Families lived in this village. They were not fighters. Even so, the soldiers attacked them. They killed nearly two hundred innocent Native people in that raid.

Trappers and Traders

People in the East heard about the animals Lewis and Clark had seen. Fur from these animals was worth lots of money. Large numbers of trappers and fur traders now began heading west.

At this time, both the United States and Britain wanted to control what is now the northwestern part of Montana. Both countries also claimed other lands in the Pacific Northwest. In 1846, they agreed to split the area. Britain took what is now western Canada. The United States took north-western Montana and nearby land. Now, the United States owned all of Montana.

Gold and Grazing Land

In 1862, gold was found on Grasshopper Creek. Hundreds of people rushed to the area. They hoped to find gold and get rich. Before long, a few lucky **prospectors** found more gold nearby. These finds brought even more people to Montana. Ranchers and farmers were among them. They raised food for the miners to eat.

Soon, thousands of people lived in Montana. It was a

rough place with few laws. Miners and ranchers often fought each other to settle their problems. The area was run by leaders who lived far away.

The people here needed a local government. To meet that need, the U.S. Congress set up the Montana **Territory** in 1864. New leaders were chosen. They passed laws that made Montana a safer place to live.

Whites Against Natives

When white settlers moved to Montana, they built their homes on Native land. The U.S. government made written agreements, called treaties, with the Natives. It paid the Natives to move to **reservations**. Soon, these reservations covered almost one-fourth of the land in Montana. Many whites did not honor the treaties. They felt free to use land that had been set aside for the Native people.

The Natives and whites began to fight. Before long, the U.S. government set up army posts in Montana.

Famous People of Montana

Mary Fields

Born: 1832, Hickman County, Tennessee

Died: 1914, Cascade, Montana

Mary Fields was born a slave. After the Civil War, she moved to Montana and became a mail carrier for the U.S. Post Office. Fields was the first African American woman ever to hold this job. She carried the mail on a stagecoach. Bandits often attacked her in the mountains, but she was a good shot with a gun. She stayed safe. She was known as "Stagecoach Mary."

In 1876, a large group of Natives was living on the Little Bighorn River. The U.S. Army wanted to make these people move to a reservation. George Custer led an attack against the Natives, but the battle did not go well for him. He and all of his men were killed. The Natives won the Battle of the Little Bighorn.

After this battle, the U.S. government sent more of its troops to Montana. In 1881, the last few Natives gave up. They were forced to move to reservations.

Good and Bad Times

In the 1870s, copper was discovered near the town of Butte. Butte Hill had such rich copper deposits that it was called "the richest hill on Earth."

IN MONTANA'S HISTORY

Here Comes the Train!
In 1883, a railroad was built in Montana. Trains began to carry copper and silver to markets far away. The railroad helped farmers and ranchers, too. Trains made it easy to ship livestock, grains, and other goods. Railroads helped Montana grow.

In the late 1800s, many people came to Montana to help build the first railroad.

Montana became a state in 1889. Before long, the new state began offering free land to settlers. The number of people in the state grew by 60 percent in ten years. Many of these new settlers were farmers.

In 1918, a **drought** struck the state. Without rain, the crops died. Some farmers left their land and moved out of Montana.

The **Great Depression** began in 1929. Prices for crops and goods fell across the nation. Many people in Montana lost their jobs, homes, and farms.

World War II and Beyond

The United States entered World War II in 1941. The war created jobs for people in Montana. Thousands of men joined the armed forces. Farmers in the state grew food for soldiers. Factories made supplies. Most of the new jobs were in places such as Billings, Missoula, and other cities.

During and after the war, coal, oil, and gas were important products in Montana. Mining made some people rich. It also left ugly scars on the land.

For many years, mining brought lots of money to Montana. Today, you can still see old mining rigs like this one in some places.

Big Sky is a well known ski resort in southern Montana. Visitors sometimes see elk and moose there.

In the 1970s, the state's leaders passed laws to protect the land. The laws made mining companies replant the land with trees and grasses.

Prices for oil and copper fell in the 1980s. Mines closed and many people in the state lost their jobs. People began to leave Montana to find work in other states.

Montana Today

Today, the state is growing again. Many tourists visit Montana each year. They spend money at hotels and tourist spots. Other types of businesses have also come to the state. Today, Montana is a fine place to live and work.

FUN FACTS

What's in a Name?

This state's name comes from a Spanish word. *Montaña* means "mountain." In fact, mountains cover only about one-third of the state's land.

1743	François and Louis Joseph de La Vérendrye explore parts of Montana for the French.
1803	The United States buys most of Montana from France as part of the Louisiana Purchase.
1805–1806	Lewis and Clark explore Montana.
1846	The United States takes control of the northwestern part of Montana.
1862	Gold is found on Grasshopper Creek.
1864	The Montana Territory is created.
1876	Natives defeat George Custer and his men at the Battle of the Little Bighorn.
1889	Montana becomes the forty-first U.S. state.
1918	A drought forces many farmers to leave Montana.
1951	Oil is discovered in eastern Montana.
1973	Laws are passed to force mining companies to **restore** land they have damaged.
2000	Montana is declared a national disaster area as wildfires burn 945,519 acres (382,638 hectares).

People

Montana is the fourth largest state in land area. In population, however, it is the seventh smallest! Only six other states have fewer people. This is a big state with a small population.

Fewer than one million people live in this state. For many years, most people in Montana lived in the country. Today, about one-half of them make their homes in cities and large towns. Billings is the biggest city in Montana. It is near the center of the state, at the edge of the

Hispanics

This chart shows the different racial backgrounds of people in Montana. In the 2000 U.S. Census, 2.0 percent of the people in Montana called themselves Latino or Hispanic. Most of them or their relatives came from places where Spanish is spoken. Hispanics do not appear on this chart because they may come from any racial background.

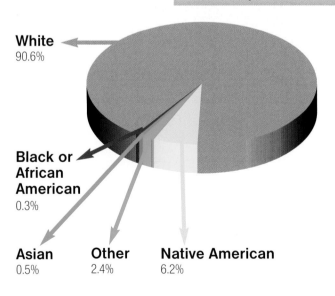

The People of Montana

Total Population 926,865

White
90.6%

Black or
African
American
0.3%

Asian
0.5%

Other
2.4%

Native American
6.2%

Percentages are based on the 2000 Census.

14

Rocky Mountains. Most of the other large cities in the state are farther west. They include Missoula, Great Falls, and Butte.

About half of all the people in Montana live in the country. They live on farms and ranches and in small communities.

Where People Came From

About nine out of ten people in this state are white. They can trace their families back to Europe. Many of them have German **ancestors**.

About 101,000 people live in Billings. It is the biggest city in Montana. Its nickname is the Magic City. When the railroad reached Billings in 1882, people said the city "grew like magic."

Some people have British and Irish ancestors. Still others can trace their roots to the countries of Norway and Sweden.

Native Americans are the next largest group of people. Still, this group is small. Only about 6 percent of all Montanans are Native Americans. Most of them

Today, many Native Americans in Montana still practice the old ways of their people. This man is a member of the Crow tribe. He is dancing at a powwow in Crow Agency.

In recent years, few people from other countries have moved to the state. Only 299 people moved here from other parts of the world in 1998. Chinese, Canadians, and Mexicans made up about one-third of these recent **immigrants**.

Religion

About one-half of the people in Montana belong to a church. Most of these people are Christian. The largest group of Christians are Protestants. Roman Catholics are next. Some

live on one of the state's seven reservations.

Few Asians and African Americans live in Montana. They make up less than 1 percent of the population.

Mormons live here. They attend the Church of Jesus Christ of Latter-Day Saints.

Montana is also home to a group of people known as the Hutterites. These people are Christians. They live simply and attend their own church. Most Hutterites live on farms and speak German. Montana has quite a few Hutterite communities.

Education

Montana has had a public school system since 1865. The first public school opened that same year. It was in Virginia City. Today, the state is known for its good public schools. Its students do well on **standardized** tests.

Montana also has a strong system of state colleges and universities. The largest of these schools is Montana State University in Bozeman.

Famous People of Montana

Crazy Horse

Born: 1842, Rapid Creek, South Dakota

Died: September 5, 1877, Camp Robinson, Nebraska

Crazy Horse was a famous Sioux Indian chief. He and his people did not want to give up their land to white settlers. For many years, Crazy Horse fought for freedom and for control of the land. In 1876, Crazy Horse and his people were living along the Little Bighorn River. The U.S. Army attacked them there. Crazy Horse and his warriors fought back. They killed George Custer and all of his soldiers in the Battle of the Little Bighorn. The Army captured Crazy Horse the next year. Soon after, Chief Crazy Horse was killed in a fight with his **captors**.

The Land

Montana is in the northwestern part of the United States. It is made up of two natural regions. They are the Rocky Mountains and the Great Plains.

The Rocky Mountains

The Rocky Mountains cover the western part of the state. They include more than fifty mountain ranges and many valleys. The highest point in the state is Granite Peak. It is 12,799 feet (3,901 meters) above sea level.

Plants and trees thrive in the valleys and on the lower slopes. Fir and pine forests cover much

Glaciers!

One part of the Rocky Mountains has been set aside as Glacier National Park. The name of the park comes from the huge sheets of ice found in its valleys. These ice sheets are called glaciers. A long time ago, the glaciers were so big that they carved the land into peaks and valleys. Today, the park contains fifty small glaciers. Melting ice from the glaciers has formed 250 lakes in the park.

Mt. Gould towers over Grinnel Lake in beautiful Glacier National Park.

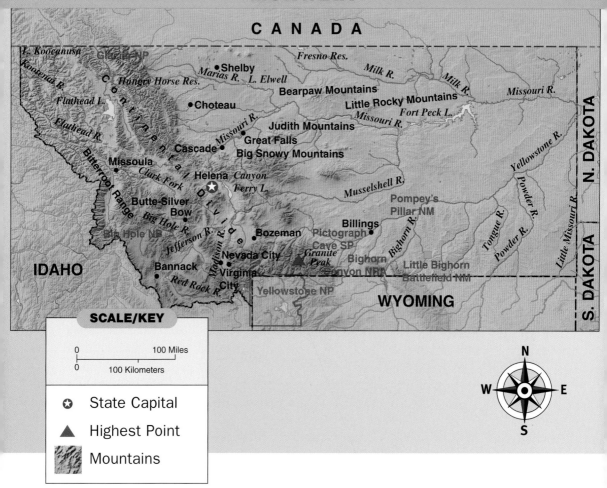

SCALE/KEY

0   100 Miles
0   100 Kilometers

⊛ State Capital

▲ Highest Point

Mountains

of this land. Animals such as grizzly bears, bighorn sheep, and moose can be seen in this part of the state. Mountain lions and elk live here, too.

One problem in this part of Montana is wildfires. In 2000, many big fires burned in the forests. Trees are now starting to grow back again in the burned areas.

The Eastern Plains

The Great Plains cover about two-thirds of the state. This region is east of the Rockies. It is filled with gently rolling hills and wide river valleys.

Grasses grow on the hills, and an open sky stretches above. This huge **expanse** of land and sky gives the state the nickname "Big Sky Country." Coyotes, prairie dogs, and deer are some of the animals that make their homes in this wide open part of the state.

Groups of low mountains jut up from the plains. The Bearpaw and Big Snowy Mountains are among them. They look like islands in a grassy sea.

The southeast corner of the state is a dry and rugged place. Over thousands of years, wind and water have carved big stone columns in the land. This area is called "the badlands."

Waterways

Montana has many rivers and lakes. The Missouri River is the longest river in

Major Rivers
Missouri River
2,466 miles (3,968 km) long
Yellowstone River
671 miles (1,080 km) long
Clark Fork River
300 miles (480 km) long

the United States. It begins in southwestern Montana and flows east all the way to the center of the country. There, the Missouri River meets the Mississippi River.

Some rivers in Montana have been dammed. Dams hold back the water in rivers so lakes form behind them. The largest lake in the state is Fort Peck Lake. It was formed by a dam on the Missouri River. The largest natural lake in the state is Flathead Lake. This big beautiful lake lies high in the Rockies.

Climate

Winds from the Pacific Ocean bring rain and snow to the Rocky Mountains. They also bring fairly warm temperatures to the valleys and lower slopes. The air grows colder, however, in the peaks. Some peaks are so high that they are covered with snow most of the year.

The Rockies block clouds as they move east. As a result, little rain reaches the plains. The plains are much drier than the mountains.

FACTS

Why Rivers Flow East or West

An imaginary line runs along some of the highest peaks in the Rockies. This is the Continental Divide. All rivers to the west of the line flow toward the Pacific Ocean. Rivers to the east of the line flow toward the Atlantic Ocean.

Montana's man-made lakes provide water for farming. Huge irrigation systems like this one bring water from the lakes to farmers' fields around the state.

Economy

In Montana, more people work in services than in any other kind of business. Service workers help other people. Doctors, nurses, and teachers work in service jobs. Lawyers, bankers, and the police have service jobs, too.

Some service workers help tourists. They have jobs in hotels and restaurants and at ski resorts and other tourist sites. Tourism makes many jobs for the people of Montana.

Making Goods

Factories provide jobs, too. Many factory workers make goods from the **natural resources** in the state. They make paper

Millions of cattle are raised in Montana. Here, cowboys drive a small herd down a road near Billings.

and lumber from wood. They process oil and coal. They make dairy products, beef, flour, and more from the farm animals and crops raised in the state.

Farms, Mines, and Forests

Ranching and farming take up about two-thirds of the land in Montana. Cattle, wheat, barley, and hay are the biggest farm products.

Today, mining is not as important in Montana as it once was. Still, the land in the state is a good source of oil, natural gas, and coal. Copper, gold, silver, and lead are mined here, too. No wonder Montana is called "the Treasure State." **Timber** from the state's forests is another kind of treasure. It is an important natural resource.

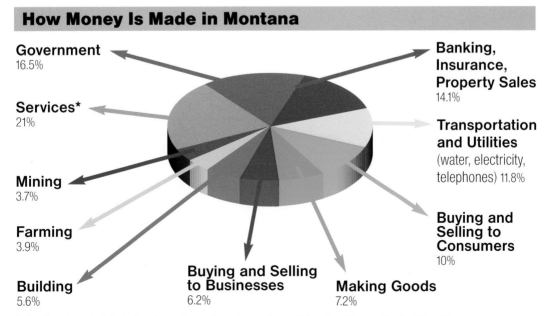

How Money Is Made in Montana

Government 16.5%

Banking, Insurance, Property Sales 14.1%

Services* 21%

Transportation and Utilities (water, electricity, telephones) 11.8%

Mining 3.7%

Farming 3.9%

Buying and Selling to Consumers 10%

Building 5.6%

Buying and Selling to Businesses 6.2%

Making Goods 7.2%

* Services include jobs in hotels, restaurants, auto repair, medicine, teaching, and entertainment.

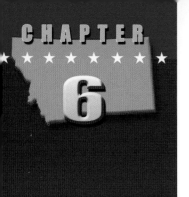

Government

Helena is the capital of Montana. The leaders of the state work in this city. The state government is made up of three parts. They are the executive, legislative, and judicial branches.

Executive Branch

The executive branch carries out the state's laws. The governor leads this branch. A lieutenant governor and a team of people known as the cabinet also work in this branch.

Legislative Branch

The legislature has two parts. They are the House of Representatives and the Senate. They make laws for the state.

The state capitol building is in Helena.

Judicial Branch

Judges and courts make up the judicial branch. They may decide whether people who have been accused of committing crimes are guilty.

State and Native governments in Montana try to work closely with each other. Native leaders met with state leaders in early 2005. After this meeting, Natives from both groups sat together and performed the Honor song.

Local Governments

Montana is made up of fifty-six counties. Most of the counties are run by three people known as the county commissioners. Towns and cities are led by a mayor or city manager and a council.

Native Governments

Montana is home to seven Native tribes. The tribes are not controlled by state laws. Instead, each tribe runs its own affairs. People of each tribe elect their leaders to make their laws.

MONTANA'S STATE GOVERNMENT

Executive		Legislative		Judicial	
Office	**Length of Term**	**Body**	**Length of Term**	**Court**	**Length of Term**
Governor	4 years	Senate (50 members)	4 years	Supreme (7 justices)	8 years
Lieutenant Governor	4 years	House of Representatives (100 members)	2 years	District (42 judges)	6 years

Things to See and Do

If you enjoy the outdoors, head for Montana! This state has truly grand mountains and plenty of wide-open space. At Yellowstone National Park, you can see wolves and elk. You can watch **geysers** shoot up from the ground, too. At Glacier National Park, you can learn how glaciers formed the Rocky Mountains. Both of these parks are awesome places to camp, hike, and learn about nature.

Montana has fun things to do all year long. In summer, the state's waterways are at their best. You can canoe, kayak, or go rafting. Fishing is great, too. You can fish

Georgetown Lake is a peaceful spot in western Montana. You can go fishing, boating, and camping there.

26

Jeannette Rankin

Born: June 11, 1880, Missoula, Montana

Died: May 18, 1973, Carmel, California

Women have not always had the right to vote. Jeannette Rankin knew this was unfair, so she worked hard to change the laws. Her work paid off. In 1914, Montana let women vote. Two years later, Rankin became the first woman ever elected to the U.S. Congress.

for trout and bass. Fall is the time for hunting. In fall, hunters head to the forests to track deer, elk, and antelope. A few months later, some people hit the trails on snowmobiles. Others strap on a pair of skis and go down-hill and cross-country skiing.

Life in Days Gone By

If you like history, stop in at Pictograph Cave National Historic Site. It is near Billings. There, you can see drawings of Native people on a buffalo hunt.

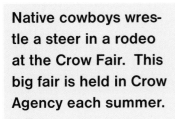

Native cowboys wrestle a steer in a rodeo at the Crow Fair. This big fair is held in Crow Agency each summer.

FUN FACTS

Buffalo Jumps

Long ago, Natives in this area did not have guns for hunting. Yet, they needed meat and hides from buffalo. To kill buffalo, Natives drove them over the edges of cliffs. The cliffs later became known as buffalo jumps. Today, you can visit buffalo jumps near Great Falls and Belgrade.

The drawings are about two thousand years old.

Pompey's Pillar National Monument is also near Billings. William Clark, the explorer, carved his name in the face of a cliff here in 1806.

Bannack was once the capital of the Montana Territory. Now it is a well known ghost town.

Today, you can still see the letters he carved in the stone so long ago.

Montana is home to some "ghost towns." Nevada City, Virginia City, and Bannack were busy mining towns. When the gold ran out, the miners moved away. Now, these towns are said to be home to nothing but ghosts.

Sports

Montana has no major league sports teams, but it has great college sports.

Famous People of Montana

Jack Horner

Born: June 15, 1946, Shelby, Montana

Jack Horner has been interested in dinosaurs for a long time. He found his first dinosaur fossil when he was eight years old. When he grew up, he became an expert on dinosaurs. In 1978, he found a nest of **ancient** dinosaur eggs in Montana. He has since found other eggs and dinosaur bones. Horner has learned that some dinosaurs lived in herds, as cows do today. His ideas have changed the way we think about dinosaurs.

Football is very popular. The University of Montana Grizzlies and the Montana State Bobcats are longtime **rivals**. These teams play each other once a year. For football fans in this state, this is the biggest game of the year.

Butte is the home of a training center used by the U.S. speed skating team. Many big speed skating events take place here.

Bobcat players and fans rejoice after the Bobcats beat the Grizzlies 16-6 in November 2005.

GLOSSARY

ancestors — family members who lived long ago

ancient — very, very old

captors — people who have caught a person or animal

drought — a long period of time without rain

expanse — wide area

fossils — bone or shells that have turned to stone over thousands of years

geysers — huge jets of hot water that burst up out of the earth

Great Depression — a time, during the 1930s, when many people and businesses lost money and farmers lost their land

immigrants — people who leave one country to live in another country

natural resources — trees, water, rocks, and other natural things that can be used by people

pelts — furs

prospectors — people who are looking for new deposits of gold or other valuable ore

reservations — lands set aside by the government for a special purpose

restore — put something back the way it was before

rivals — people or groups that compete against each other

standardized — the same for everyone

territory — an area of land that belongs to a country

timber — trees that are cut to use for building

Books

B Is for Big Sky Country: A Montana Alphabet. Discover America State by State (series). Sneed B. Collard III (Sleeping Bear Press)

Crow Children and Elders Talk Together. Library of Intergenerational Learning (series). E. Barrie Kavasch (PowerKids Press)

Montana. Rookie Read-About Geography (series). Lisa Trumbauer (Children's Press)

The Story of "Stagecoach" Mary Fields. Stories of the Forgotten West (series). Robert H. Miller (Silver Burdett)

Yellowstone National Park. Symbols of Freedom (series). Margaret Hall (Heinemann)

Web Sites

Enchanted Learning: Montana
www.enchantedlearning.com/usa/states/montana/

Go West Across America with Lewis and Clark
www.nationalgeographic.com/features/97/west/

Montana Kids' Site
www.montanakids.com

A Raptor Named Bambi
www.wmnh.com/wmbam000.htm